THE
POET'S WAY OF
KNOWLEDGE

BY

C. DAY LEWIS

C.B.E., M.A.

*Sometime Professor of Poetry in the
University of Oxford*

THE HENRY SIDGWICK
MEMORIAL LECTURE, 1956

CAMBRIDGE
AT THE UNIVERSITY PRESS
1957

1105

ONCE upon a time poetry and science were one, and its name was Magic. Magic, for our earliest ancestors, was the most effective way of understanding nature and their fellow-men, and of gaining power over them. It was not till some three centuries ago that science finally broke away from magic: the scientific revolution of the seventeenth century withdrew from the 'supernatural' as a field of study; and if science since then has led to other varieties of superstition, we must blame, not the scientists, but the layman, who finds superstition a difficult thing to live without. The course of poetry has been different. If the first great pre-scientific hypothesis was animism, and the first great pre-scientific method was imitation, then poetry, in so far as it still rests upon imitation and animism, must seem a very primitive procedure.

Nevertheless, I believe poetry to be a possible way of gaining and imparting knowledge—a son of the same father as science: the brothers may quarrel from time to time, but each in his own field they are working towards compatible ends. To define the field of poetry should make it clear in what sense we may claim that poetry is concerned with knowledge. This I shall try to do. And I shall also suggest that there are remarkable affinities between the method of the scientist and the method of the poet—between the ways their minds work, particularly at one crucial stage of their investigations.

Although no one has ever succeeded in defining poetry, there have been many praiseworthy attempts to say what poetry is *for*. These have always been bounded by two extremes—the idea of poetry as an end in itself, and the idea of poetry as a means. In the 1890's, for example, reacting no doubt against the prevalent utilitarianism of their day, poets proclaimed 'Art for Art's sake'. Poetry should be a ritual, a mystique, detached from morality, from the factual and the topical, from any religious preaching or scientific teaching: its job was to be beautiful, and useless. The young Yeats could deplore 'that brooding over scientific opinion which', he believed, had 'extinguished the central flame in Tennyson'. And it is noticeable that this manifestation took place at a time when science, flushed with a century of practical success, had got rather above itself and was claiming the whole world of knowledge, achieved or potential, as its own. Let me quote from a popular handbook of science first published in 1892:

There is no short cut to truth, no way to gain a knowledge of the universe except through the gateway of scientific method. The hard and stony path of classifying facts and reasoning upon them is the only way to ascertain truth. It is the reason and not the imagination which must ultimately be appealed to. The poet may give us in sublime language an account of the origin and purport of the universe, but in the end it will not satisfy our aesthetic judgment, our idea of harmony and beauty, like the few facts which the scientist may venture to tell us in the same field.

4

No wonder, faced with such a deluge of complacency, there was a scramble for the summit of pure poetry. To the passage I have just quoted—and it does not represent the scientific attitude today—one might reply like this: Let us suppose that, not a 'few facts', but everything there is to be known about the oceans had been discovered by hydrographers, marine biologists and the rest; and let us suppose that psychologists and neurologists had arrived at a complete comprehension of the workings of the human mind; and let us suppose that some artist-scientist, some Leonardo, had incorporated all this knowledge in a lucid and commanding book: would that book 'satisfy our aesthetic judgment, our idea of harmony and beauty' more fully than they are satisfied by *The Ancient Mariner*? I doubt it. Would that book supersede *The Ancient Mariner*? I am quite sure it would not.

'Well, of course it wouldn't', you may say: 'the two works are not comparable: the one is a poem of pure imagination, whereas the other would be an assembly of observed facts and verified laws, of knowledge about real things.' Certainly: but are you implying that poetry is not concerned with 'real things'? Is not the feel of a thing as real, as much a fact, as the thing felt? Is not the conveying of the quality or value of an experience, therefore, a contribution to knowledge no less useful than the analysis of that experience in terms of physical fact and natural law? Coleridge's poem, through images of ocean travel, tells a story of guilt, retribution and expiation—a sequence of events no less actual than the sequence of events which produces coal gas. Any psychologist would agree, I think, that the mental events symbolised in the poem are true to observed facts of human behaviour. But the poem does not merely embody a complex of experiences; it *is* an experience: and thus the kind of knowing it offers is different from the knowledge we should get from a number of case-histories illustrating the same sequence of mental events.

If we reject the idea of poetry as nothing but an end in itself, we shall see it as a means towards a special kind of knowing. What is this 'special kind of knowing' we claim for poetry? Poetry, they tell us, gives us a keener awareness of life. Such definitions are lamentably vague. But attempts at greater precision have not proved much more satisfactory. These can be summed up under two general headings: the idea that poetry improves us, by showing us images of perfection—'the end of all earthly learning being virtuous action', or, as Bacon put it, 'Poesy serveth and conferreth to magnanimity, morality, and to delectation'; and the idea that poetry is a way of penetrating through appearances to the heart of reality. The former leans upon Aristotle's definition of poetry as *mimesis*, imitation; the latter, towards poetry as the re-ordering and re-creation of experience: here we have, respectively, the traditions of mimetic and of symbolic magic.

The common factor is, of course, pleasure. And critics have theorised for centuries about the nature of the pleasure which poetry gives. I. A. Richards, for

6

example, who based his critique on the profoundly romantic principle that 'experience is its own justification', explained the pleasure we receive from poetry in terms of psychic balance. 'We must picture...the stream of the poetic experience as the swinging back into equilibrium of these disturbed interests.' A poem a day keeps the psychiatrist away. Richards distinguishes between the statement of science and the pseudo-statement of poetry: the latter, he says, 'makes us remember how we felt'; it operates in a field which is closed to science. 'Language logically and scientifically used cannot describe a landscape or a face.' Mr T. R. Henn has spoken of the moral value of art as the 'sensitizing of the human mind to the living world and its complexities'; 'the final justification of all poetry', he says, is 'that it seeks to express a peculiar fusion of ideas and emotions which are normally on the edge of consciousness, or even beyond it.'

But, for the most eloquent justification of poetry by a contemporary, I might go, not to any poet or critic, but to a great mathematician. Here is what A. N. Whitehead wrote:

The soul cries aloud for release into change. It suffers the agonies of claustrophobia. The transitions of humour, wit, irreverence, play, sleep, and—above all—of art are necessary for it. Great art is the arrangement of the environment so as to provide for the soul vivid, but transient, values.

But, he goes on,

great art is more than a transient refreshment. It is something which adds to the permanent richness of the soul's self-attainment. It justifies itself both by its immediate enjoyment, and also by its discipline of the inmost being. Its discipline is not distinct from enjoyment, but by reason of it.... The fertilisation of the soul is the reason for the necessity of art.

'The soul cries aloud for release into change.' Set that beside Yeats's lines, 'Man is in love and loves what vanishes. What more is there to say?', and you get one of the great paradoxes on which poetry is based.

Let us descend now from this rarefied atmosphere and see if, by means of a parable, or pseudo-statement, we may more sharply distinguish the poet's way of knowledge from the scientist's. I will ask you to imagine Wordsworth on a motor-tour of the Western Highlands with a young scientist called Jones—an anthropologist. I must also ask you to forget, for the time being, the actual origin of Wordsworth's *The Solitary Reaper*. Well now, driving through a remote glen, they see a girl, all by herself in a field, wielding a sickle. It is very picturesque. Jones stops the car, for a better look. He and Wordsworth become aware that the girl is singing —a tune they have never heard, in an unfamiliar mode.

'I wish I knew what she's singing,' says Wordsworth.

'Why not ask her?' says Jones. 'No. Wait a minute.' Jones, you see, is a conscientious scientist: the girl may not speak English, he thinks; she may not know the name of the song, or her evidence may be inaccurate.

'Look here, Wordsworth,' he says. 'I'll just just run back to the hotel and fetch my tape-recorder. You hold her in conversation till I get back.'

Wordsworth's capacity for holding country folk in conversation is, of course, notorious. All goes well: the tape-recorder is fetched, the girl induced to repeat her song. Jones notices, while she is doing so, that Wordsworth has gone back to the car and is holding his hands over his ears: the behaviour-patterns of poets really are unpredictable.

Jones got his recording, and having submitted it to musical experts, learnt that it was a Jacobite lament, in Gaelic, previously unknown. His curiosity stimulated, he presently returned to the neighbourhood of the glen and put in several months' hard field work. He found there an isolated pocket of earlier civilisation almost untouched by modern communications. The girl, for instance, was reaping that field with a sickle, alone, in accordance with an ancient belief that to do so would ensure fertility in a young bride. The Jacobite lament had got superimposed upon this much more primitive custom as a result of the Young Pretender's having made a brief sojourn in the glen, in the course of which he begot several children. Jones set out his findings in an article contributed to a learned periodical: the article was entitled 'Some Notes towards a Survey of Residual Culture-Patterns in the Western Highlands of Scotland'. This article started a lively correspondence: a fellow-anthropologist, for instance, wrote to tell Jones that he had observed curiously similar fertility-rites in the Trobriand Islands. Gradually, a mass of facts was accumulated. Brooding over these, Jones one day in a flash of illumination perceived a certain thread running through them, relating them. Cautiously, perseveringly he tested it: the thread held firm. He had discovered a law. Jones' First Law, as it is called, is familiar to all anthropologists, and I need not trouble you with it.

Meantime, Wordsworth also had made his contribution to knowledge. It, too, is familiar:

> Behold her, single in the field,
> Yon solitary Highland Lass!
> Reaping and singing by herself;
> Stop here, or gently pass!
> Alone she cuts and binds the grain,
> And sings a melancholy strain;
> O listen! for the Vale profound
> Is overflowing with the sound.
>
> No nightingale did ever chaunt
> More welcome notes to weary bands
> Of travellers in some shady haunt,
> Among Arabian sands:
> A voice so thrilling ne'er was heard
> In spring-time from the Cuckoo-bird,
> Breaking the silence of the seas
> Among the farthest Hebrides.
>
> Will no one tell me what she sings?—
> Perhaps the plaintive numbers flow
> For old, unhappy, far-off things,
> And battles long ago:
> Or is it some more humble lay,
> Familiar matter of today?
> Some natural sorrow, loss, or pain,
> That has been, and may be again.

Whate'er the theme, the Maiden sang
As if her song could have no ending;
I saw her singing at her work,
And o'er the sickle bending;—
I listened, motionless and still;
And, as I mounted up the hill,
The music in my heart I bore,
Long after it was heard no more.

A contribution to knowledge? Yes. 'Art is concerned with uniqueness, science with generality'; and, as Yeats said, 'Nothing unique is measurable'. For Jones, the girl in the field became one fact in a heap of similar facts whose discovered relationships finally led to the great generalisation known as Jones's First Law. We remember Wordsworth's moral distaste for scientific ideas—for their abstraction, the way they seemed to leave out everything that was most important. Wordsworth's task was to show, not similarity, but uniqueness—the uniqueness immanent in a commonplace experience. His concern is not even with the girl as an unique individual, so much as with the state of mind she produces in him. The knowledge we get from the poem is knowledge of a certain mood; and this is the mood of 'Man is in love and loves what vanishes'. Each of us has experienced this sense of revelation, or at least of profound significance trembling on the edge of revelation, which some chance encounter inspires. We want the encounter prolonged until we have extracted its full meaning; but only art can stabilise the passing experience, the fleeting mood, into something both momentous and permanent. 'The Maiden sang As if her song could have no ending.' But every song has to end: although its life may be protracted for a while— 'The music in my heart I bore, Long after it was heard no more', the unique quality of the experience it gives can survive only as a dwindling memory, unless it is fixed, developed, printed in a work of art.

We imagined Wordsworth returning to the car and holding his hands over his ears when the song was re-sung. The poet's trained instinct had told him that he must hear no more: the germ of a poem was already at work in his mind, and further factual knowledge might endanger it. How significant it is that his first version of the line, 'I listened, motionless and still,' was 'I listened, *till I had my fill*'. Just as it was necessary for Jones to find out what the girl was singing, so, for Wordsworth, it was essential *not* to know. Look at the structure of the poem. Stanza 1 states the physical facts. Stanza 2, with its images of nightingale and cuckoo, enlarges those facts by giving us the tone and thrill of the experience. In stanza 3 we concentrate upon its essential meaning; and it is done, you notice, by asking questions to which the answers must remain for ever unknown—was the song about 'battles long ago', or some 'familiar matter of today'? Had Wordsworth followed his 'Will no one tell me what she sings?' with seven lines informing us that it was a Jacobite lament, we might still have had a good poem: but it would have been quite a different poem, because it would be giving us knowledge of a different state of mind; and it would have required a resolution of the theme other than the one we get in stanza 4, where the poet returns to the physical facts, charged now with the emotional meaning that has been generated in stanzas 2 and 3.

Here is a poem, then, which offers us knowledge of a particular state of mind—one that the poet experienced originally, but that the sensitive reader may to some degree share with him through the poem.

Certain objections may now arise. The crudest would be this: 'But I don't *need* knowledge about my feelings or my states of mind: they are mine: if I know anything at all, I know them.' This is like a man saying, 'Oh but I live in Suffolk, so I don't need to look at Constable's paintings.' Next, a more serious objection: a chemist might argue,

'A chemical experiment in accordance with a given formula, provided it is correctly carried out with adequate equipment, will invariably produce the same result through the same sequence of events. That predictability is what *I* mean by knowledge. You may talk of a poem as a controlled experiment; but its results are unpredictable—no two readers respond identically to a given poem: it is wrong to give the name "knowledge" to so variable a set of responses.'

I do not think this argument is very sound. Though competent readers (and I do not mean literary critics only) might differ on the meaning of particular passages in a poem, there is unlikely to be any wide divergence between them in respect to its general tenor. Even if there were, it would not greatly matter: must uniformity

13

of response be a condition of every kind of knowledge? Individuals, because they are each unique, will within certain limits interpret differently the unique events we call a poem: but their responses have one thing in common—the conviction of truth, a sense that the poem has enabled them to *know* more clearly, more deeply or more passionately.

But apart from this, the enlightened scientist today will *not* equate knowledge with predictability: he is more likely to say, 'there is a probability amounting to a certainty that the result of a given experiment will be x'. For instance, if you put several hundred tons of ammonium nitrate in a dump, there is a probability, amounting to a certainty, that they will stay quiet: but there have been one or two cases where dumps of pure ammonium nitrate have spontaneously blown up. It may have been, of course, that the ammonium nitrate was not, as it was believed to be, pure. But it is also possible that some *unpredictable* grouping of random micro-events occurred, to render the mass unstable. Now until recently the scientist has sought for general laws governing macro-events, and has drawn from them inferences about individual events. Whereas the poet generally seeks first for knowledge of the individual micro-event and its relation to the macrocosm: that is one thing Coleridge meant when he said that a poem is an organic growth from within outwards. But, during the last half-century, physical scientists have moved towards the study of the micro-event: this has brought them nearer to the poets, and brought them up against the realisation that there is an irreducible limit to what can be known by observation about even the smallest event in isolation from all other events. Heisenberg's Principle of Uncertainty says that there is a limit to the knowledge we can gain about a micro-event in isolation, because in order to observe it we have to do something to it, and thus to change it. Both the scientist and the poet are concerned to diminish as far as possible the area of uncertainty. Wordsworth, stopping his ears when the girl was singing her song again, did so in order to preserve intact and precise his sensations on first hearing her—in order not to widen the area of uncertainty. So, a physicist will evacuate a tube to study the behaviour of the electrons in it, unconfused by the presence of gas atoms. He and Wordsworth are both selecting from the sum total of 'real' conditions.

A third objection to poetry as knowledge is based on perception. We know what we do know through our senses. Science is concerned with the perceptible world: poetry, though it uses material of the perceptible world, is concerned with the imperceptible. But the imperceptible admits of no examination, no proof; therefore no activity within the field of the imperceptible can claim to produce knowledge. This—the materialist argument—has been rendered obsolete by modern physics. Let me quote from Martin Johnson's *Art and Scientific Thought*:

Now much of the concern of the modern physical scientist, atoms, electrons, atomic nuclei, electron-waves, etc., is essentially not of a nature to be directly known to

15

sight, touch, or hearing. These 'things' are as far from being objects of direct sense-perception as anything imagined by the most fantastic of artists. If the latter justifies himself by the coherence of the communicated ideas to which his patterns give rise, where is he resembling and where is he differing from, the physicist whose view of the universe is a deliberately woven structure of ideas which also radically diverges from sense perception?

This, coming from a scientist, puts the whole problem of scientific knowledge and poetic knowledge on a different, a much sounder basis. Elsewhere Mr Johnson writes, 'It becomes profitable to regard art and science as each attempting to communicate mental images through patterns and structures and forms, in the qualitative domain of feeling and in the quantitative domain of measurement respectively'. And again, 'The test of the validity of the scientist's "pattern" of ideas is that its form must render it communicable'. The distinction between qualitative and quantitative defines the separate fields of science and poetry: the emphasis on communicability shows the common interest of the two. If you still like to think of science as 'knowledge', and poetry as at best some kind of 'pseudo-knowledge', no one can stop you, but you will be thinking in terms unacceptable to many scientists today. Here, for instance, is what a biologist, Professor J. Z. Young, says:

...in our specialized society there are many individuals who contribute to the whole by the study of the means of communication itself—artists, writers, critics, and thinkers, for example. We can describe their activities also in objective language. The creative artist is an observer whose brain works in new ways, making it possible for him to convey information to others about matters that were not a subject for communication before. It is by search for means of communication that we sharpen our powers of observation. The discoveries of the artist and scientist are exactly alike in this respect.

As I understand it, perhaps the greatest problem now facing those sciences which cannot use the language of mathematics is the problem of finding a language more efficient to communicate their ideas. It is a problem greatly complicated, even for the mathematician, by the principles of Relativity, which demand that a statement about any course of events should admit the modifications necessary if it is to be equally true for any other observer stationed anywhere or moving in any direction at any speed. In the writings of scientists we frequently come across such phrases as 'Physiologists have no generally accepted way of talking about' so and so. They tell us that the exact *description* of their thoughts is part of the discipline required for discovery: if we could find the right way to describe a given process, we should know more about the process. It is here that the affinity between poetic method and modern scientific method is most striking. The poet today, like the scientist, thinks of his work as a kind of exploration. Not all poets in all their poems, but at least many poets in many of their poems, are aiming to relate and clarify their experiences, to arrive at greater self-knowledge. The poet's problem of communication is this: he wishes to communicate something to himself; if he succeeds in doing so, he will also communicate something—though not precisely the same something—to the reader. He is unlikely nowadays to think of poetry as an imitation of nature, of human actions and virtues: he sees it rather as a re-ordering of experience, or as a process by which the symbolic value of his memories is discovered.

I would not want you to forget what is often lost to sight among the ramifications of critical theory—the poet as a maker. Absorbed in the pure but not simple craft of verse, in the extreme pleasure and pain of making a poem, he will become temporarily unaware of the searcher after knowledge who stands at his elbow. The poet is still, above all, a maker: but, for good or ill, his mind does seem committed to a more insistent self-consciousness and a greater degree of complexity than many of his predecessors shared: one sign of this is the number of poems written nowadays which are in effect poems about the poetic sensibility and the poetic act.

The initial stage of making a poem is often a kind of groping in the dark. Consider the possible ways in which a poem such as *The Solitary Reaper* might be conceived. The poet may first become aware of a certain poetic form, its structure and rhythms, insistently haunting his mind—a song without words, which demands of him that he find the words for it. Or he might simply say to himself 'I've been writing a great deal of blank verse this year: I need a change: what about some rhyming eight-line stanzas with four beats to the line?' Or a phrase out of a book he is reading makes him prick up his inward ear. Or a line of poetry comes to him, full-fledged, out of the blue. He may find himself arrested by a snapshot in a photograph album, or pondering some past episode which has suddenly presented itself to him with a look of singular complicity. The clue, the donnée, whatever it be, may have a self-evident bearing on what happens to be preoccupying the poet at the time; or it may seem to have none at all.

The poet fixes this clue as bait on the end of his line, casts it into the sea of his experience, and in a watchful passivity waits for whatever may attach itself to the bait. What is he fishing for? Memories, images, phrases. Many come up; and most of them have to be thrown back into the sea, because they are misleading, or unsuitable, or irrelevant. To what? To the pattern just beginning to take shape in the poet's mind—a pattern still only hinted at, which will reveal the theme of the poem. Let us suppose that the subject of the poem is a girl cutting corn in a field, alone, singing to herself. The poet has to discover what this subject means to him: the experience, whether first-hand or second-hand, embodied in this subject could allow many interpretations: the interpretation finally offered by the poet is the theme of the poem.

We are compelled to speak of the poetic process in metaphor. At this early stage, the poet has begun to build a house with only one small part of the blue-print available to him, or while he is still drawing the blue-print, or with many alternative blue-prints at his disposal. If he has to work in this hand-to-mouth way, it is because conception and form are for him inseparable, because a poem is an organic growth in which the theme only reveals itself through the growing pattern. 'How can I tell what I mean till I see what I say?' Most poems which go wrong, go wrong through the poet's failure to extract the right theme, or extract it whole, from his subject-matter. His activity during the initial stages of making a poem is equivalent to what Professor Young calls 'doubt' in scientific investigation: it is a rigorous questioning of data—data which include the poem's original subject, the secondary subject-matter which is attracted into the field of the poem out of the poet's whole life-experience, and the formal patterns into which he is beginning to arrange it. This questioning is, for the poet as for the scientist, an arduous intellectual exertion. He must justify himself, as Martin Johnson puts it, 'by the coherence of the communicated ideas to which his patterns give rise'. Coherence is achieved formally by the pattern of rhyme and metre, the correspondences of phrasing and imagery. But formal coherence is vain unless it is coherence round a well articulated theme: the latter alone can give poetic meaning to experience, and thus communicate a unique state of mind.

In this questioning, language is of supreme importance. Poets are compelled to break away from the language of their predecessors, a poet may be compelled to alter his own style radically, because language is the instrument of poetic investigation and quickly grows blunt. If we write in the style of Herrick, say, or Browning, we shall find ourselves feebly reproducing

Herrick's or Browning's state of mind. If I have perfected a language of my own, I may have to discard it because its very perfection induces facility—the poet's greatest danger: a much-used idiom, like a well-worn path, will lead the poet's steps insensibly away from the theme he should be searching for, to some familiar and exhausted one. It is a paradoxical truth that the poet needs his instrument, language, to resist him if it is to cut deep and disclose some new, living aspect of whatever themes are implicit in his experience.

I have spoken of the early stages of a poem as a kind of groping in the dark. I want you now to consider three quotations:

(i) ...the state of imaginative muddled suspense which precedes successful inductive generalisation.

(ii) There were no particular questions that I asked myself: there were no special objects upon which I directed my mind: there was only a formless and aimless intellectual disturbance, as if I were wrestling with a fog. I know now that this is what always happens when I am in the early stages of work on a problem. Until the problem has gone a long way towards being solved, I do not know what it is.

(iii) For him...the ultimate synthesis of a design was never revealed in a flash; rather he approached it with infinite precautions, stalking it, as it were, now from one point of view, now from another, and always in fear lest a premature definition might deprive it of something of its total complexity.

Those three quotations, which could be luminously

describing the conditions at the start of a poem, are in fact from A. N. Whitehead, from the philosopher and historian R. G. Collingwood, and from an essay on Cézanne by Roger Fry. 'The state of imaginative muddled suspense', the 'formless and aimless intellectual disturbance, as if I were wrestling with a fog'—how gratifying it is to the poet, that a mathematician and a philosopher should start in a muddle, just as he does. 'Until the problem has gone a long way towards being solved, I do not know what it is': exactly—until the poem has gone a long way towards being written, *I* do not know what *it* is. And Cézanne's careful 'stalking' of his design, his fear 'lest a premature definition might deprive it of something of its total complexity'—how often my own impatience has sent a poem off at half-cock, so that it missed its proper theme, or only scored an outer on it.

That 'stalking' metaphor brings to mind the legend of Bellerophon and Pegasus. Bellerophon, you remember, spent a whole day, exerting all his strength and science to catch the winged horse. All day it eluded him. That night, as he slept, he dreamed that the goddess of Wisdom had given him a golden bridle. Waking, he found the bridle beside him, and Pegasus at once submitted his neck to it. So the poet must exercise all his skill if he is to capture his theme and mount upon its inspiration. But the skill and devotion are not in themselves enough: without them, he would indeed never be given the magic bridle; one may think of the bridle as a charm woven from his skilful though unavailing

22

manœuvres to catch Pegasus. But, however devotedly he has used his resources, the bridle still may not come to him. He needs luck, too—the favour of the goddess.

Is not this legend true, not only for the discoveries of the artist, but for those of the scientist, the historian, the philosopher? They, too, must do a great deal of spade-work before the imaginative leap becomes possible; and no amount of spade-work can guarantee that a leap will be made; and when it *is* made, it is often a leap in the dark, or, if you like, *from* the dark—the mathematician Poincaré getting the solution of a problem as he stepped into a cab thinking about other matters, or Kekulé, while riding on top of a London bus, suddenly seeing the carbon and hydrogen atoms, already known to be in the hydro-carbons, join hands to form a long chain, and later seeing them in a dream dance round to join hands again and thus form the benzene ring. The poet's recognition of his theme may seem instantaneous, but it is the end of a gradual process, just as the scientist's recognition of the relationship between recurring sequences of facts has been preceded by the amassing, the orderly classification and the severe scrutiny of those facts. And one point more; it is unwise to equate scientific activity with what we call reason, poetic activity with what we call imagination. Without the imaginative leap from facts to generalisation, no theoretic discovery in science is made.[1] The poet, on the other hand, must

[1] 'Copernicus found that the orbits of the planets would look simpler if they were looked at from the sun and not from the

not only imagine but reason—that is to say, he must exercise a great deal of consciously directed thought in the selection and rejection of his data: there is a technical logic, a poetic reasoning in his choice of the words, rhythms and images by which a poem's coherence is achieved.

Similarly we must be careful to avoid thinking that, whereas poetry is a language based upon metaphor, science always gives us direct, unvarnished, prose statement. The fact is that all languages, except that of the mathematician, have frequent recourse to metaphor. The scientist speaks of electric charges 'attracting' or 'repelling', of matter 'obeying' certain laws. He finds such animistic expressions convenient. But he will use metaphor and analogy, as the poet does, not only for expressing but for discovering. Let us compare the nervous system to a clock and see what this tells us, said Descartes. Let me compare my love to a red, red rose, and see what follows, said Burns. The modern biologist compares the human brain to an automatic pilot, a telephone-exchange, a sorting-office, a government department: he even goes to the electronic engineer and says, 'Build me an automatic brain. It may teach me something about the workings of the human brain.' Professor Young tells us, of such analogies, 'The point is that comparing something unknown with something already known makes it possible to talk about the un-earth. But he did not in the first place find this by routine calculation. His first step was a leap of imagination—to lift himself from the earth and put himself wildly, speculatively into the sun' (J. Bronowski).

known. The value of making the analogy is that it facilitates communication.'

This is equally true for the communications of science and of poetry. But of course there is a fundamental difference between their attitudes towards analogy and metaphor. In a poem, metaphors cannot contradict or cancel one another: they can only blur one another. When they fail, it is because they have failed to make for coherence of pattern. If a poetic metaphor is right, it is always right. A scientific metaphor, on the other hand, like a scientific law, is valid only as long as it covers the known facts, illuminates them, and offers the most effective way of talking about them.

'Where our knowledge halts, our description will resort to metaphor', said Sir Charles Sherrington. This could be taken by the simple-minded as an argument that poetry is not knowledge—or, by the perverse, that much scientific description is a kind of poetry. I should be perverse enough myself to agree with the latter proposition, up to a point. But, at least if we substituted 'knowing' for 'knowledge', I do not think Sherrington would have quarrelled with my claim for poetry. 'The "I"', he wrote, 'can never come into the plane of objects of sensual perception. It *is* awareness....But the mind does experience itself. Memory attaches to that experience. The self can remember and re-live.' Poetry, I have suggested, can be a record of the mind experiencing itself, and thus a way of knowing better, of understanding, our moods, feelings, passions. In an eloquent passage of his Gifford lectures, Sherrington wrote this:

Mind, for anything perception can compass, goes therefore in our spatial world more ghostly than a ghost. Invisible, intangible, it is a thing not even of outline; it is not a 'thing'. It remains without sensual confirmation, and remains without it for ever. Stripped to nakedness there remains to it but itself. What then does that amount to? All that counts in life. Desire, zest, truth, love, knowledge, 'values'....

I have tried to point out certain affinities between the scientific and the poetic approach. I shall now move on to still more debatable ground. What use, if any, can the poet make of scientific theory or applied science? In Wordsworth's preface to the second edition of *Lyrical Ballads*, there are two well-known passages. First, 'The poet writes under one restriction only, namely, the necessity of giving immediate pleasure to a human Being possessed of that information which may be expected from him, not as a lawyer, a physician, a mariner, an astronomer, or a natural philosopher, but as a Man'. Second, 'The remotest discoveries of the Chemist, the Botanist, or Mineralogist, will be as proper objects of the Poet's art as any upon which it can be employed'—this seems to conflict with what Wordsworth has just said, but he goes on—'if the time should ever come when these things shall be familiar to us, and the relations under which they are contemplated by the followers of these respective sciences shall be manifestly and palpably material to us as enjoying and suffering beings'.

26

I do not think that literary criticism or aesthetics, since Wordsworth's time, have produced any more definitive statement upon this point. Scientific knowledge must have become common knowledge before the poet can use it: for example, as a contemporary critic more boldly puts it, there needs to be a 'total assimilation of Freud's discoveries of a kind which allows the writer *to be no longer aware that he is using them*'. The scientist might well protest that such a use would mean over-simplification and distortion, but we must for the moment ignore his protests. We must also exclude from this discussion the mere versifying of scientific information: no one is likely nowadays to write a poem on the lines of Erasmus Darwin's *Lives of the Plants*. But most poets are stimulated by the ideas of their age, and all must respond to the climate of their times. Ours, as everyone tells us, is a scientific age; and scientific theory has relaxed the rigid mechanism which so appalled Tennyson when he tried to come to terms with science. It should be not only possible but rewarding for poets now to approach the body of material which scientists have accumulated.

In doing so, however, they are faced with two difficulties. First, the body of material is so vast, demanding ever narrower specialisation. No one could aim, as Humboldt did 150 years ago, to represent the whole of the physical aspect of the universe in one work. A thing of the past, too, is that hopeful amateurism which allowed Alan Sedgwick to get himself elected in 1818 to the Woodwardian Chair of Geology in this University, while admitting total ignorance of the subject. 'Hitherto,' he said, 'I have never turned a stone: henceforth I will leave no stone unturned.' How can the poet today derive any cosmology from science, when the scientific experts themselves are each working within a narrow and seemingly self-contained field? Yet, if the poet's field is the human mind and its values, and men's minds are so widely affected by modern scientific theory and technology, the poet must in his own explorations take account of this changing country through which he moves. He will be better able to do so, perhaps, if he shares the scientist's view of Nature as operating through inexorable laws of necessity, indifferent to Man's notion that he is a special case—the view which caused Whitehead to declare, 'the pilgrim fathers of the scientific imagination as it exists today are...Aeschylus, Sophocles, Euripides'.

The poet's second difficulty is a technical one, and was hinted in that passage from Wordsworth's preface. If, as poets did in the 1930's, he tries to use for metaphor 'the remotest discoveries of the Chemist, the Botanist, or Mineralogist', he is in danger of falling into shallow conceit. Until the constructions of modern technology become naturalised objects in landscape and townscape, it is very hard to assimilate them into a poem, for they lack connotation—lack, so to speak, that depth of soil, accumulated by long periods of sensuous and emotional reference, in which poetry may strike roots. No doubt a poem drawing some analogy with the internal-combustion engine would be more likely to communicate something to the Common Reader than a poem using metaphor of atomic fission. But poets must still walk a long way behind the technologists for their gleanings and meanings. With scientific theory, the problem is even more awkward. Poetry on the whole requires a stable foundation of ideas from which to make its flights: but today, and particularly in the all-important field of physics, there seems to be a constant modification and readjustment of scientific theory.

Nevertheless, that scientific ideas can be assimilated into poetic knowledge is shown by poems of Edwin Muir, William Empson, Kathleen Raine, and others of our day. Analogies from the sciences have proved useful, also, in literary criticism. Professor George Whalley, for example, in his illuminating book, *Poetic Process*, proposes the analogy of 'the interface' to illustrate the several attitudes towards reality of the poet, the mystic, the scientist and the common man. Sherrington had used the term 'interface' to describe the surface of our planet 'where phases solid, liquid and gaseous meet', and where 'special opportunities for interaction occur'. Professor Whalley asks us to 'imagine that man and nature (or "subject" and "object") meet and embrace each other at an inter-face'; that 'life, naked living, occurs at this interface... it is here that man meets and shapes "nature" and is himself shaped by nature.... All values cluster at the interface and are not to be found elsewhere.... To be "involved" at the interface is to be "real", to engage

29

in reality'. The purpose of the poet, Professor Whalley suggests, is 'to reveal "what it is like" at the interface'.

I myself find this parable, of which I have not time to give more than a cursory sketch, an extremely helpful way of talking about poetry. 'Reality' is a precarious word; but sooner or later, in discussing the field and purpose of poetry, one cannot avoid it, for if poets are not concerned with the exploration of 'life, naked living', at its most intense, and with giving us the feel of it, then I do not know what they *are* up to. Their task is to show the momentousness of life's most common-place happenings; and it is a task all the more important at a time when man and his planet have dwindled into physical insignificance against the immense distances of space and time which science has revealed. As a recent writer puts it, 'There is no immutable law to say that scenes which have been enacted on a puff of star-dust in a moment of time should have any ultimate significance'. If it is only through religion that we may be *convinced* of the ultimate significance of the human scene, poetry and the other arts can at least give some of us a *sense* of its significance, its momentousness.

It is here, perhaps, that poetry may best act nowadays as corrective and complementary to science. When science tells us that the galaxy to which our solar system belongs is so enormous that light, travelling at 186,000 miles per second, takes between 60,000 and 100,000 years to cross from one rim to the other of the galaxy, we laymen accept the statement but find it meaningless—beyond the comprehension of heart or mind. When

30

science tells us that a human being contains '1000 billions of unit principles, each of which lives' or that 'the human eye has about 137 million separate "seeing" elements spread out in the sheet of the retina', we are no less paralysed, intellectually and emotionally. Man is appalled by the immensities and the minutenesses which science has disclosed for him. They are indeed unimaginable. But may not poetry be a possible way of mediating them to our imagination? of scaling them down to imaginative comprehension? Let us remember Perseus, who could not look directly at the nightmare Gorgon without being turned to stone, but could look at her image reflected in the shield the goddess of Wisdom lent him.

Certainly, the pictures which science shows to man of the universe he lives in, and of the universe within himself, offer the most amazing material for the poet to meditate upon. It would be a sad thing if no poets could be found to dwell upon it and give it imaginative meaning. Whether the poet is attempting these heights and depths, or is giving significance to life's commonplaces, poetry still involves some kind of animism, some projection of self into the so-called 'inanimate' world. This projection will take subtler, more self-conscious forms, no doubt—

> The red rose cries, 'She is near, she is near':
> And the white rose weeps, 'She is late';

—it's a long way from that to T. S. Eliot's

> for the roses
> Had the look of flowers that are looked at.

31

But Eliot with his sophisticated roses and Tennyson with his romantic ones are each giving us knowledge of a certain state of mind.

Early in my lecture I quoted from a handbook of popular science of 1892. Let me now quote from a book of popular science published last year: in his *A Guide to Earth History*, Richard Carrington writes: 'Science, art and religion, evolving to new insight from their starting place in the mind of primitive man, are inseparable processes. They are all techniques of knowledge, operating with equal validity at different levels of awareness.' If we think of poetry thus, as a technique of knowledge, we shall help break down the artificial and indefensible barriers between science and poetry which, alas, our modern educational system still tends to maintain. And we shall also answer, or rather put into the discard, that other question with which I began— poetry, means or end? Every poet knows that his poem is both an end in itself and a means to further discovery. 'To treat life in the spirit of art', said Walter Pater, 'is to make life a thing in which means and ends are identified.'

This Henry Sidgwick Memorial Lecture, delivered in Newnham College, Cambridge, on 27 October 1956 by C. Day Lewis, C.B.E., M.A., was published in 1957 by the Syndics of the Cambridge University Press and printed in Great Britain at the University Press, Cambridge (Brooke Crutchley, University Printer).